THE BUSHCRAFT HANDBOOKS

TRAPS & SNARES

Illustrations by the Author

Richard H. Graves

The Bushcraft Handbooks
Traps & Snares

This Edition Copyright © 2013 by Palmer River Publishing

Cover, Graphics and Layout by: Palmer River Publishing

ISBN-13: 978-1484822265
ISBN-10: 1484822269

About The Author

The author of "The Bushcraft Handbooks", Richard Graves, is a member of the Irish literary family of that name. A veteran of the Great War campaigns in the Dardenelles and the Western Front, the author became passionate about the bush at an early age. As an enthusiastic bushwalker, skier and pioneer of white-water canoeing, he foresaw how a knowledge of bushcraft could save lives in the Second World War. To achieve this end, he initiated and led the Australian Jungle Rescue Detachment, assigned to the Far East American Air Force. This detachment of 60 specially selected A.I.F. soldiers successfully effected more than 300 rescue missions, most of which were in enemy-held territory in New Guinea, without failure of a mission or loss of a man.

An essential preliminary for rescue was survival, and it was for this purpose that the notes for these books were written. These notes were later revised and prepared for a School in Bushcraft which has been operating for several years and continues to provide valuable instruction to Servicemen embarking overseas on active service in Korea and Malaya.

Bushcraft

As far as is known, "The Bushcraft Handbooks" are unique. There is nothing quite like them, nor is any collection of published bushcraft knowledge as comprehensive.

The term "Bushcraft" is used because "woodcraft" commonly means either knowledge of local fauna and flora or else is associated with the blood-sports of hunting and shooting. "The Bushcraft Handbooks" include a volume on traps and snares, but these are purposely-designed to be completely ineffective for native animals which are insect enters or grazers. These traps have been included because they would only be effective in catching predatory animals such as cats and dogs which have taken to the bush, and other "pest" creatures such as feral swine or goat.

"Bushcraft" describes the activity of how to make use of natural materials found locally in any area. It includes many of the skills used by primitive man, and to these are added "white man" skills necessary for survival, such as time and direction, and the provision of modern "white man" comforts as illustrated in the volume on bush campcraft.

The practice of bushcraft develops in an individual a remarkable ability to adapt quickly to a changing environment. Because this is so, the activity is a valuable counter to the over-specialisation so prevalent in today's society, and is particularly significant in youth training and character-moulding work.

INTRODUCTION to the BUSHCRAFT HANDBOOKS

THE PRACTICE OF BUSHCRAFT shows many unexpected results. The five senses are sharpened, and consequently the joy of being alive is greater.

The individual's ability to adapt and improvise is developed to a remarkable degree. This in turn leads to increased self-confidence.

Self-confidence, and the ability to adapt to a changing environment and to overcome difficulties, is followed by a rapid improvement in the individual's daily work. This in turn leads to advancement and promotion.

Bushcraft, by developing adaptability, provides a broadening influence, a necessary counter to offset the narrowing influence of modern specialisation.

For this work of bushcraft all that is needed is a sharp cutting implement: knife, axe or machete. The last is the most useful. For the work, dead materials are most suitable. The practice of bushcraft conserves, and does not destroy, wild life.

R.H.G.
April, 1952

CONTENTS

About The Author iii

Bushcraft iii

INTRODUCTION to the BUSHCRAFT
HANDBOOKS v

TRAPS & SNARES 1

Simple Snares 3

Ground Snares 4

Tree Snares 12

Logfalls 14

Bow Trap for Guarding a Path 19

Thrower 21

Pig Stabber 22

Box Traps to Catch Animals Alive 23

Portable Box Traps 24

Wire Cage Trap for Rabbits 29

Net Trap for Catching Animals Alive 29

Use of a Rat-Trap or a Fish Hook for
Ducks or Geese 30

Blind Roller for an Automatic Fisherman 31

Fish Traps 32

Improvised Fish-Hook Made From Thorns 39

Fishing Spears 39

Baited Float Stick 40

Tracks, Baits and Lures 41

TRAPS & SNARES

The ability to pick up a couple of dead sticks from the ground, and with a sharp knife and a little know-how produce a practical and workable release for a snare or trap is a valuable exercise in improvisation and inventiveness. As far as is known this the first time a collection of improvised releases and with this snares and traps has ever been published. Some of these are potential man-killers, developed by soldiers in jungle warfare to protect themselves. The knowledge of these possible man-killers must be treated with as much respect as a loaded firearm.

They are included because they could be lifesavers for man stranded in hostile country.

The snares and traps shown are far more humane than the vicious steel-jawed devices which clamp onto a wild creature's leg, inflicting severe pain, creating panic in the captured animal, and hold it prisoner until it finally dies from pain, hunger or exhaustion.

Conservationists may condemn releasing the knowledge of how to make the mechanics for these snares and traps, implying that this will inevitably mean destruction of local wild life.

This is not correct, in practice the opposite is the truth.

None of the traps are killers. The wild animal is caught alive and unharmed. Most people, after examining the captive, feel that it is too interesting to destroy (unless it is itself a destroyer), and will release it unharmed. More often than not the snares and deadfall, which are humane killers, will be used to capture the "pest" creatures, dogs and cats which have gone wild and are the biggest killers of local bird life, rabbits, foxes, and other "vermin" animals. These are the "scavengers" which are the real destroyers upsetting the balance of nature in a locality.

Two cardinal rules are: never set a trap which might injure anyone without first putting up warning signs in the area, and never leave a trap or snare set, and then forget about it. Some wild creature may be caught in it, and if it is a trap, suffer hunger needlessly.

The following traps and snares are but a few of the many which you can improvise with a little ingenuity. The releases and principles are comparatively few in number, but the variations are infinite. When making your trap or snare, make it sufficiently strong to hold the animal when it is caught. You must put good workmanship into traps or they are likely to be ineffective. It is far better to spend an extra hour in work to make the trap secure and strong, rather than try and save an hour by thinking that a flimsy erection will suffice.

Knowing the animal which you are hoping to trap will enable you to decide whether to set the release 'fine' or whether to set it 'tough,' so that the animal will have to tug and worry the bait, and thereby become bold and unsuspicious.

Included in these traps are a few which could be exceedingly dangerous to man. These are given because they are very little known, and could possibly be of great value to explorers or others. Several of these man-killers were devised during the War in the Pacific by men who were adrift in the jungle and used these 'automatic sentries' to make their camps safe from attack by hostile natives or enemy forces.

Some of the traps are illegal in certain countries, and the trapper should acquaint himself with the local game and trapping laws.

The type of trap you must make depends largely upon the animal for which it is being set, and the local conditions. Only experience can guide you in deciding which trap or snare will serve you best.

Simple Snare

Snare set over rabbit burrow.

Snare set in path, held in position with twigs.

This is merely a running noose set either in the entrance to a burrow or other hiding place of the animal, or else set across one of its paths. The noose should be of some strong material; fine brass wire (picture wire) is probably about the best. The brass is stiff enough to bend easily into shape, the noose will stand by itself, and being very thin it will probably not be seen by the animal, and yet it is strong enough to hold the snared creature captive. One end must be very securely fastened to a peg or other reliable anchor.

If fine wire is not available for noose snares, cord can be used, or if this not available it can be spun, plaited, or twisted from local fibrous material.

Generally when cord is being used it will be necessary to hold the noose spread open. Very thin twigs can be used for this purpose. They should be set lightly in the ground, and have just enough strength to hold the noose open. Remember that the snared animal has sharp teeth and therefore the ability to chew its way out of the snare if given time. Wire obviously is difficult for the animal to bite, but with cord there is no difficulty, and an animal can release itself in a few minutes if it does not panic and struggle forward into the noose, as so often happens. When you set the noose snare it must be visited regularly at short intervals.

Snare set in ajimal path.

Ground Snare

TOGGLE AND BAIT STICK RELEASE

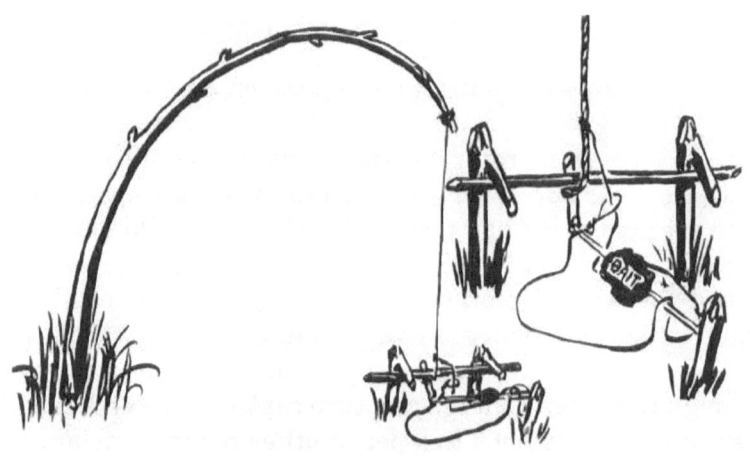

Select a site where there is a springy sapling. Lop the sapling of its branches and top. Bend the sapling over, and make a mark on the ground under the head of the bent sapling. This is the place where you will set the sticks for the

4

snare. Cut two hooked stakes. These should be sharpened at the point, and bevelled at the head so they will drive easily into the ground. They must be straight and strong, and preferably cut from dead wood. The hooks should be about two to three inches above ground level. Between the two hooks, and about twelve inches in front of them an anchor peg is driven into the ground. Three straight sticks for the release are selected. One must be long enough to go between the two forks and lie under them. The other is only about three inches long and is the toggle stick, and the third, which is about twelve inches long, is the bait stick. A stout cord is tied to the head of the lopped sapling, and the sapling itself is bent so that the head is over the two hooked stakes. Where the cord from the head of the sapling touches the cross stick the toggle stick, is tied securely, and above it another cord is tied and formed into running noose.

The toggle stick is passed in front of the stick between the two hooked sticks, and under, so that the cord lies hard against the front side cross stick.

The lower end of the toggle stick presses against the bait stick, which in turn presses against the anchor peg. The noose is laid over the bait stick.

When the animal touches the bait stick, it frees the toggle stick, and the upward spring of the sapling, acting swiftly, draws the noose round the captive bird or animal.

This snare should not be left set for more than twelve hours at a time. If the sapling is kept bent for too long it will lose its springiness, and render the snare ineffective.

An alternative release may be effected by using two forks driven in at such an angle that the cross stick is pulled against the lower side of the fork.

The setting of the noose may be varied for certain types of ground feeding creatures so that the noose, instead of lying flat on the ground, over the bait stick, is held vertically so that the animal or bird must put its head through the noose to reach the bait.

TOGGLE AND BAIT STICK RELEASE

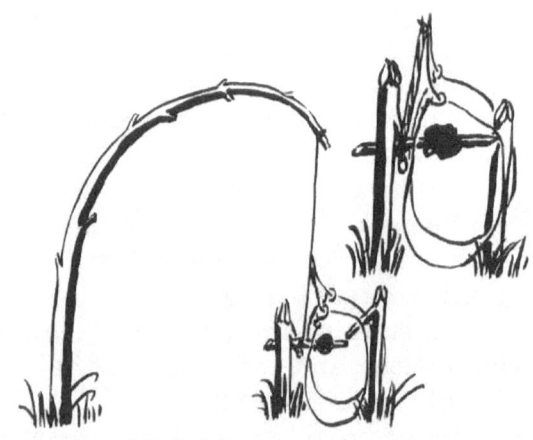

In this snare a springy sapling is lopped of its top and branches. Two strong hooked stakes are cut, and one with a shorter hook is driven into the ground directly beneath where the head of the sapling comes when it is bent over. At right angles to the hook of this stake, the other hooked stake is driven into the ground. It should be about one foot distant. The cord for the snare is tied to the head of the sapling, and the noose made in another cord tied just above the free end. The free end is tied to the bait stick, which held beneath the fork of one stake, is pulled upwards against the prong of the hook of the other stake. Setting can be varied in sensitivity by narrowing down the edge of the hook against which the bait stick is pulled. Noose, or nooses should be vertical and spread a few inches away from the bait, so that the animal must put its head or forequarters inside the noose to reach the bait.

This snare should be released after about twelve hours of setting to restore the springiness to the sapling.

REVERSED TOGGLE BAIT STICK RELEASE

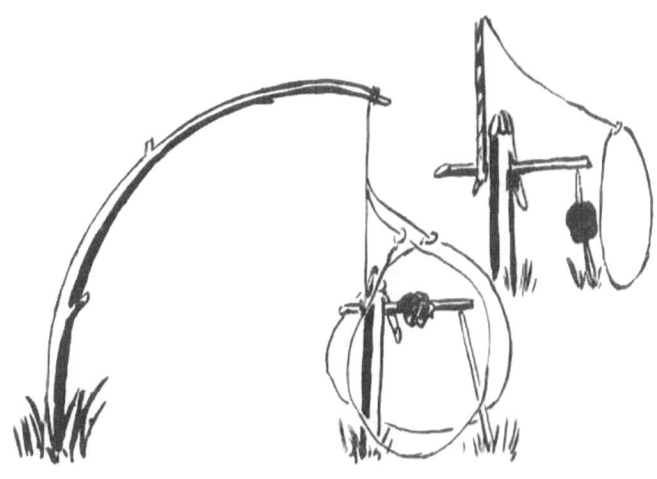

A whippy sapling, trimmed of its top and branches to reduce the weight, is bent over, and directly beneath its head a very stout hooked stake is driven into the ground.

A strong cord is tied to the head of the sapling, and the other end of the cord is tied an inch or so from one end of a toggle stick some eight to ten inches long. This long end of the toggle stick is passed under the fork of the hooked stick (see sketch). The bait may either be placed on this toggle stick, or alternatively on the stick which it presses to the ground.

A noose is tied to the cord above the tie of the toggle stick, and brought forward, and held in position by thin twigs (not shown) so that it is a few inches in front of the bait stick. If the toggle stick is used to carry the bait it is advisable to put out two nooses, one on either side of the bait.

Care must be taken to see that the long end of the toggle stick is short enough to pass freely under the hooked stick. If the toggle stick is too long it will simply smack down on the ground and jam the release. It must be short enough to swing completely free under the hook.

STEPPED BAIT STICK RELEASE

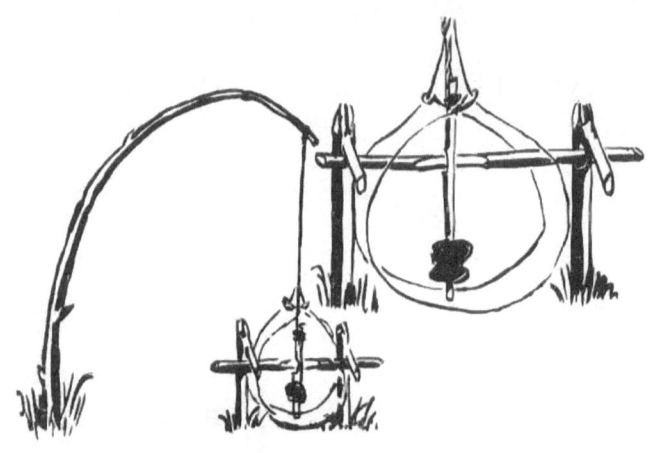

A whippy sapling is trimmed of its branches and head, and bent over. Note the point on the ground which will be directly under the head when the snare is set.

Two strong hooked stakes are driven into the ground about nine inches apart. A cross stick is roughly squared in the centre and placed beneath the two hooks with one of its squared faces directly facing the ground. The bait stick is cut with a cleanly cut faced step, the bottom of the step is on the lower end of the cut. To the top end of the stick the cord from the sapling is tied securely (a clove hitch or stopper hitch is good for this purpose).

One, or better still, two, nooses are run out from the main cord, and held vertically a few inches from the baited end of the stick by thin twigs (not shown). An animal touching the bait disturbs the seated laces, and releases the stepped bait stick which holds the bent sapling. Sensitivity of the release is effected by the 'grip' of the seated face of the bait stick.

NICKED BAIT STICK RELEASE

A whippy sapling, lopped of top and branches, has a stout cord tied to its head. The sapling is bent over, and directly beneath the lopped head, a strong hooked stick is driven into the ground. The end of the hooked side is sharpened to a chisel point.

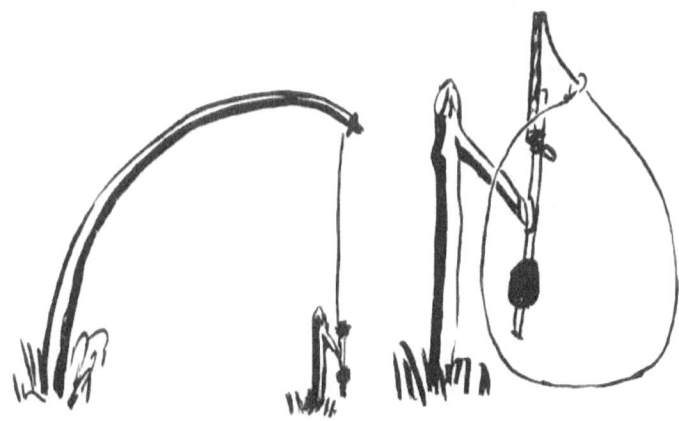

The bait stick is cut with a square nick so that this will engage the chisel edge of the hook. The cord from the head of the sapling is tied to the top end of the nicked bait stick, and the bait is secured on the lower end.

From this cord the noose is tied, and spread a few inches in front of the baited stick.

Fine setting is obtained by making the nick shallow, or for a stubborn release cut the nick deeply.

CROSSBAR BAIT SNARE

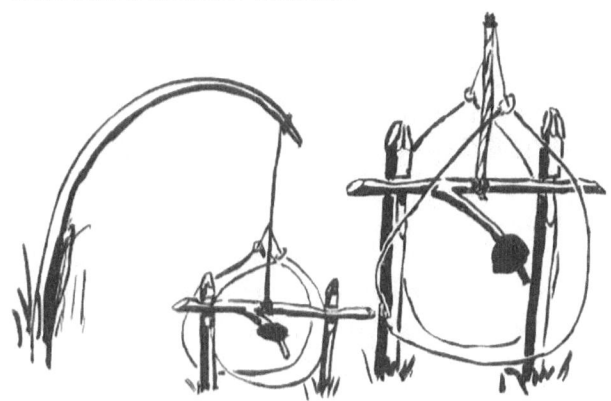

Two stout straight stakes are cut. On the upper end of each a nick is cut, with the straight step on the top end of the stake. The cross bar is now cut, with a side branch so that the end of the side branch is a few inches away from the cross bar. The side farthest away from the side branch is squared on top and sides to fit the squared faces of the stakes. A whippy sapling, lopped of its branches and top, is bent over so that it comes directly above the head of the two stakes driven into the ground. A cord from the head of the sapling is tied to the centre of the cross bar. The side branch is baited, and two nooses are spread either side of the baited crossbar.

Depth of cuts into the two stakes affects the degree of sensitivity of release.

DOUBLE ENDED FIGURE FOUR SNARE

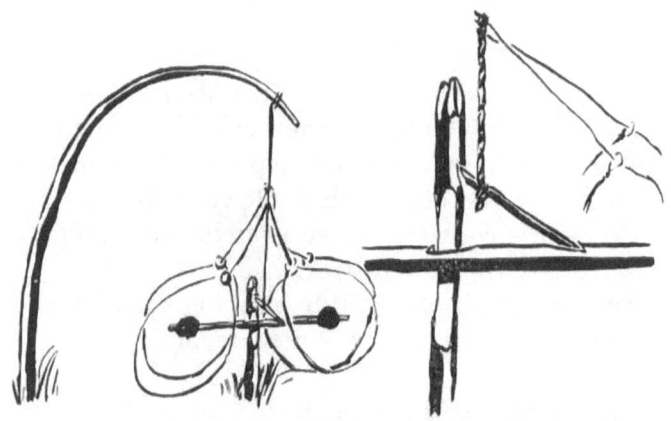

A whippy sapling, trimmed of its branches and head, is bent over and the site directly beneath the head marked on the ground. Before releasing the sapling a stout cord is tied to the head. The three sticks for the release are now cut. One of these is a stake. It must be sharpened at the point, and bevelled at the head. About eight inches from the head two sides are squared off at right angles to each other, and about three inches below the head an undercut nick is made in one of the sides opposite to one of the squared sides.

The crossbar bait stick is now cut. This may be two feet long. In the centre it is nicked or cut to provide a squared step less than one-quarter inch deep. On the end farthest from this step, and at right angles to it, an undercut nick is made. The toggle release stick is now cut. One end is sharpened to a chisel edge, and put in the undercut nick in the stake. The crossbar is placed with its step against the squared edge of the stake, and the undercut nick facing to the top. Mark on the toggle stick where the end should be cut to sit in the upper nick of the crossbar, and sharpen the toggle stick to a chisel point. Tie the free end of the cord from the sapling head to the toggle stick, and then tie on cord for four nooses, and set same in position with forked twigs.

A DOUBLE SPRING SNARE

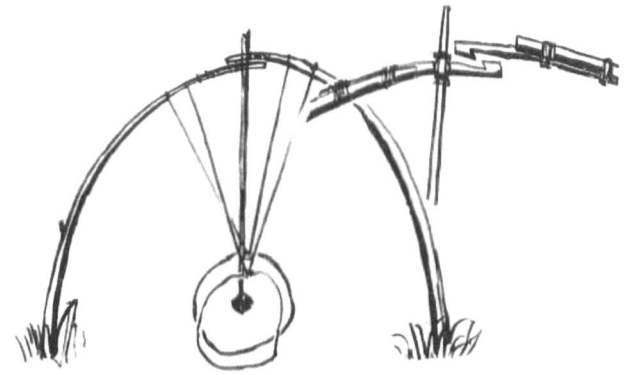

Two saplings are trimmed and bent towards each other. At their heads two interlocking sticks are tied. These sticks are cut so that they step into each other. The bait stick is lashed to one of these, and four cords for the nooses (two onto each sapling head) are lashed.

The snare is set bending the two saplings over, locking the two sticks together, and then setting the nooses, two on each side of the bait, and a few inches distant.

When the animal disturbs the bait, it twists the interlocking sticks, and so releases the two saplings. In springing apart they pull the nooses against each other, and hold the captured animal securely.

TRACK SPRING SNARE

A site is selected on an animal trail where a tall sapling is available a few feet to one side of the track. The sapling is lopped of its branches and top, and a stout cord is tied to the head. Where the bent sapling crosses the trail tall stout pegs are driven well into the ground on either side of the track. To the tops of these stakes a cross bar is securely lashed. There may be occasions when convenient trees will serve instead of stakes.

A stout cord or rope is tied to the head of the sapling and a few feet along the cord a thin strong stick is tied. This stick should nearly reach from the crossbar to the ground. The cord from the sapling is tied a few inches below one end. This end is placed under the crossbar, and the lower end which will now pull forward strongly with the pressure of the bent sapling's spring, is laid against a thin cross-stick. The noose of the snare is lightly tied to the top crossbar and the stakes to keep it spread open. Release is effected when the animal touches either the bottom stick, knocking it down, or the toggle stick with the cord. Either action will release the holding down of the sapling, and it will spring upright, tightening the noose around the animal's neck.

Tree Snares

SIMPLE NOOSE FOR TREE CLIMBING ANIMALS

NOTE—This snare is prohibited in many areas, and should not be used unless absolutely necessary, and only where its use is permitted.

A site is selected by examining a tree which shows the claw marks of tree climbing animals on its bark. The 'lean' of the tree is carefully examined, and on the upper side of the 'lean' a stout straight pole eight to ten feet long, and at least three or four inches thick is placed to make a 'path' for the animal from the ground to well up the tree trunk. The animal will use this pole to climb the tree on its nightly excursions. Onto the upper end of the pole set a simple wire noose, fastened securely to the pole itself.

The animal in climbing or descending the pole will put its head or paw into the noose, and so ensnare itself.

Note.-A point of interest is that most tree living animals will descend a tree if the base of the tree is consistently beaten with a heavy instrument such as the back of an axe or a heavy club. Nocturnal animals will descend a tree in broad daylight, but the blows must be continued and fairly heavy. It is probable that the animal feels the shock through (lie tree and, obeying an impulse to quit before the tree falls, leaves its hiding place. This is an excellent method of getting night feeding animals into daylight for photographing.

NOOSE SNARE STICKS FOR SMALL BIRDS

NOTE.—This is a prohibited snare, illegal in many districts. It should not be used except to catch pests.

A straight stick three to four feet long is selected. Onto this many fine nooses, each between ½" and 1" in size, of horse hair are tied securely and the stick is then tied with the nooses uppermost to a shrub or small tree which is a favourite resting place for small birds. They alight on the stick, and their feet become entangled in the snares. One or two birds so caught will call others to them, and in a short time seven or eight birds will be all snared on the noose stick.

This type of snare stick is condemned for general use. It has a place for the orchardist to clear starling and fruit eaters from his orchard, but it should not be used to snare small birds such as finches and wrens for the purpose of putting them into captivity. If you see such a stick, obviously set for such a purpose, take it and destroy it. You will be doing the birds a good turn by this action.

Logfalls

SLIP RELEASE OF BAIT STICK

This logfall is suitable for ground living animals, and depends for its action upon the turning or twisting of a forked bait stick, one end of which is sharpened to a point which in turn supports the smoothly cut face of the cross bar on which the logs are lying. Select a site where the animals feed. Cut your bait stick with a widely forked prong. The lower end should be roughly sharpened, and the top end brought to a sharp point. A stout stake is sharpened and bevelled at the head so that it is nearly flat. This stake is driven securely into the ground. The two or three heavy logs for the fall are selected and trimmed so they will lie together on the cross bar. The cross bar is cut with a squared side at one end, and the other end is trimmed off with a smoothly inclined face. The squared side is laid on the top of the bevelled stake. The logs are laid on the cross bar, and the sharpened point of the bait stick is put under the inclined cut on the end of the cross bar at such an angle that it will slip off if the bait stick is twisted. The lower end of the bait stick rests on a chip of bark or a smooth flat stone so that it will not sink into the ground. Sensitivity is adjusted by the angle of the bait stick on the cut at the end of the cross bar.

SQUARED FACE RELEASE OF BAIT STICK

The general construction of this logfall release is similar to the slip release. A stout stake is sharpened and driven into the ground as for the preceding trap. The cross bar, except for two squared sides in place of the smoothly cut inclined end is exactly the same. The bait stick is forked and at the upper end a square seated cut is made to take the squared side of the cross bar, so that when the weight of the logs is resting on the cross bar the squared side is securely resting on the square cut at the top end of the bait stick. When the prong with the bait is disturbed the bait stick is twisted, and the crossbar unseated so that the logs fall on the animal beneath, either breaking its back instantly or crushing its head so that death is immediate.

FIGURE FOUR RELEASE

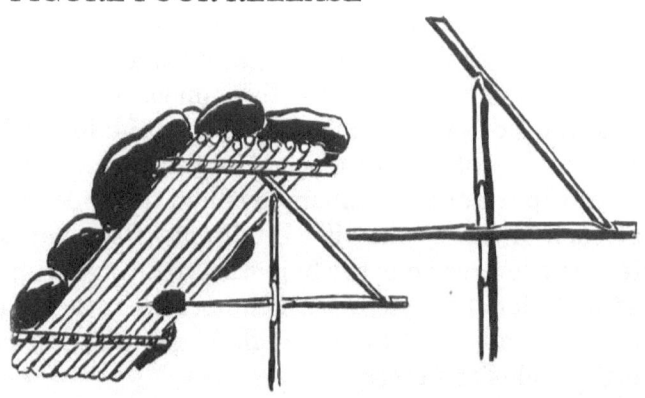

In this type of logfall the two or three heavy logs are bound to cross pieces at head and foot so that they will lie together. Alternatively a platform of light sticks weighted with heavy stones can be made. Release is effected by the Figure 4 method. For this release three strong sticks are selected, one about two feet high for the upright, one about three or four feet long for the bait stick, and one about eighteen inches for the release stick.

The upright is sharpened to a chisel edge at the top, and twelve inches below this and facing the same direction as the straight edge of the chisel end the stick is squared off on two adjacent sides. The bait stick is cut with a nick sloping backwards a couple of inches from the thickest end, and about twelve inches further along with a squared step, the squared side of which is farthest away from the nick. The bait is at the far end of the bait stick. The release stick is sharpened to a chisel edge at either end, and a nick parallel to the chisel edge is cut some few inches from one end. Setting of the trap is effected by standing the upright stick a few inches from the end of the logs. Lifting the logs and putting the release stick under the cross bar, with the chisel cut of the upright in the nick in the release stick. The far end of the release stick is seated in the nick at the end of the bait stick so that it draws the square face of the cut against the squared face of the upright stick. Any disturbance of the bait releases the logfall.

TOGGLE RELEASE

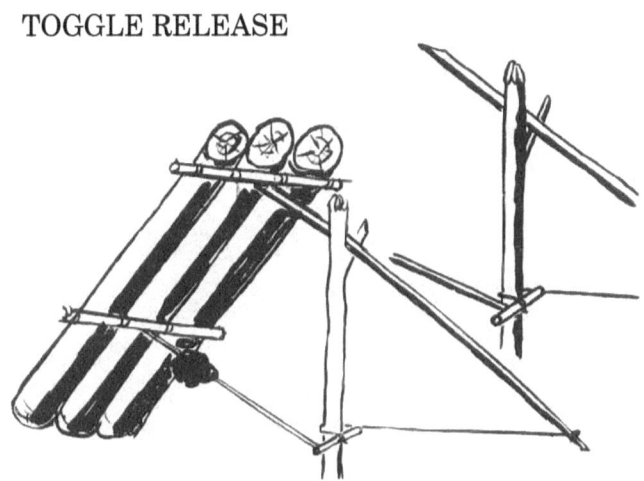

Two or three logs are secured to a cross bar as for the figure 4 release. The release sticks consist of a forked stick about two feet long for the upright, a support stick about three feet long, a toggle stick of four or five inches, and a bait stick, long enough to reach from the upright stick to the lower cross bar holding the logs together.

The trap is set by standing the upright with the fork uppermost a few inches in front of the logs. The support stick is laid over the fork, and to its farthest end a cord is tied. The length of the cord should reach from the end of the support stick to the upright stick. The end of the cord is fastened to a toggle stick and this is passed around the upright. Against one end of the toggle stick the bait stick is placed so that its farthest end presses against the lowest cross bar. Release is effected when an animal disturbs the bait stick, and so releases the toggle, allowing the logfall to drop.

In place of a group of logs for any of these traps, a platform of stakes, heavily weighted with big stones, may be used with equal efficiency.

TREE LOGFALL

NOTE—This is an exceedingly dangerous trap. It is so absolutely unsuspected and sudden that it should only be used either to guard against surprise from attack if in a country of hostile natives, or if set to kill large animals. Notices of warning: should be placed at either end of the path. This trap is a man-killer.

A site is selected along a trail which the animals use regularly. The site must have a branch of a large living tree overhanging the path. A heavy line is thrown over the branch so that when allowed to hang free its end will lie on the path. To this line a stout rope is tied and the rope hauled up and over the branch. To one end of the rope a heavy log is slung so that it hangs horizontally.

The log is hoisted to the branch, and the rope brought back so that it is concealed by the tree trunk; a toggle is tied where tire rope touches the ground. At this place two very strong hooked stakes are driven into the ground, and a release similar to any of the noose releases (toggle and bait or reversed toggle) are used to hold the rope.

To what would be the bait stick in the snare release, lengths of cord or ground vine are tied for a trip cord and by means of hooked sticks the trip cord is led through the bush parallel to the animal's path to positions on either side of the place where the log will drop when it falls. This distance can be calculated by allowing for the log to fall at the rate of 28 feet the first second, 56 the second, and 28 feet more for each further second, and so on. (Drag on the cord reduces the log's rate of fall to this figure.) If the animal travels at three miles an hour, it moves forward 4 feet 6 inches a second. Thus, if the dog is 100 feet above the path it will take two and a half seconds to fall and the animal will have moved 11 feet 6 inches after it has pulled the trip with its feet.

After setting this trap it should be given a test drop and, if satisfactory, reset only after placing warning notices several yards either side telling people to pass around the area, and not under any consideration to pass along the track. Failure to provide these notices might easily lead a careless person into gaol for manslaughter.
Remember this trap is a potential man-killer.

Bow Trap for Guarding a Path

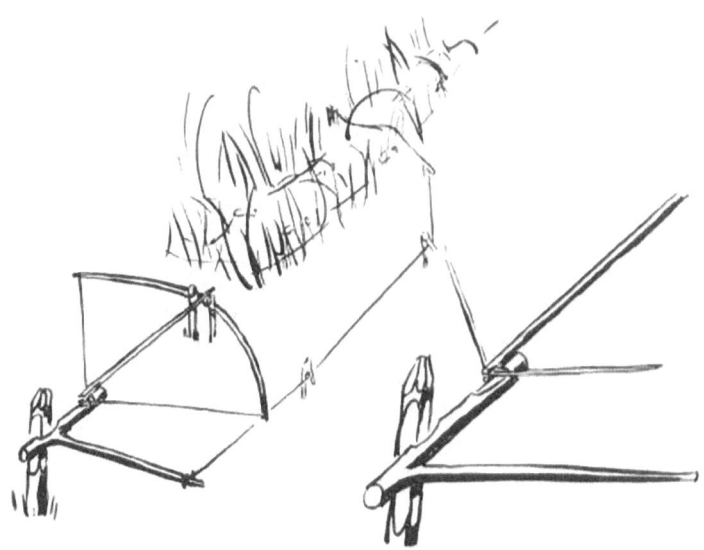

This is an extremely dangerous trap, and a certain man-killer if the bow is strong and the trap properly set. It should not be used except in cases of emergency.

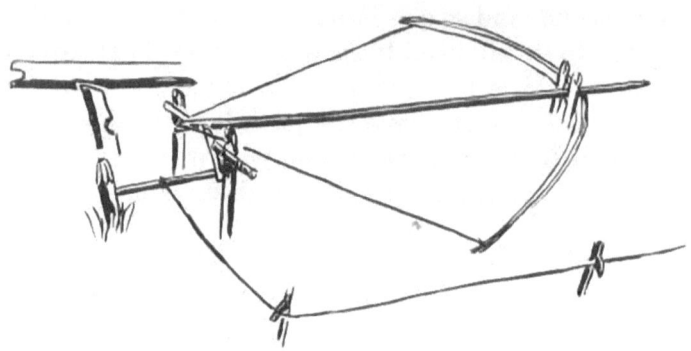

A bow of considerable strength is made, and lashed to two stakes driven securely into the ground. The two stakes are set an inch or so apart. At right angles to the bow, and at the position where the bow string will come when the bow is drawn, a third stake is driven into the ground. The horizontal angle between the lower end of this peg and the place where the bow is lashed to the twin pegs should be such that the arrow will be given correct elevation to catch the man or animal at a vulnerable height when the trip cord is touched. The site should be at the bend of a trail or path.

Release can be effected by a hooked stick which has a square nick cut on the outside edge of one side, and at right angles to this cut a reversed nick is cut to take the bow string. The rear peg is squared at its rear and on one side to form a right angle. The squared cut of the release stick engages the squared face of the stake, and the thong is hooked over the undercut nick, so that the bow is held drawn back to the rear peg. The arrow notch is in the thong. Release is effected by tying the release cord to the other end of the hooked stick and leading the release cord through the grass or bush to a position at the edge of the path. Guiding of the cord is effected by means of inverted hooked sticks. At the path the release cord is tied to convenient growing material such as a wisp of grass, a ground vine, or even a casual stick.

An alternative release is effected by deeply nicking with a square face the underside of the arrow. Into this nick a chisel edge release toggle stick is engaged. The release stick passes in the rear of a short cross bar so that the forward-pull of the bow pulls the lower end of the release stick to the rear. This lower end is pressed against a trigger stick which is pushed against an anchor peg. To this trigger stick the trip cord is tied and from here it is led through the bush to the path, and set as a trip cord across the trail in the same manner as the hooked stick release.

A WORD OF WARNING . . . remember that this trap is a man-killer. Never ever leave it set and unguarded unless to defend yourself. Place warning signs on the path.

Thrower

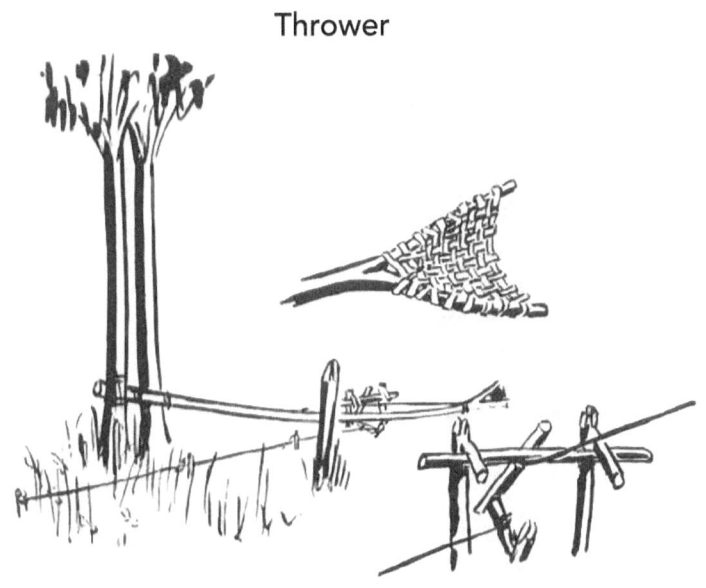

There may be occasions when it is desired to create a diversion on one side of a path in order to frighten animals or people moving along the path away from it and into an ambush. For this purpose a thrower can be set up at a convenient distance from the path so that when a trip cord is touched the thrower will hurl a stone or other missile onto the path, and so drive the animal off the path and towards the hunter.

A forked springy sapling is lashed between two trees as for the stabber. The end of the sapling is forked, and in the forked end a shallow pouch is woven between the forked sticks. These forked sticks should be at an angle of about 45 degrees from the horizontal towards the path. The sapling is bent back and down and secured as for the stabber, and about four feet short of the place where the head came when it was at rest a very stout stake is driven into the ground to act as a 'stop' to the forward thrust. The sapling must be lashed fairly high up the two trees and bent downwards to the securing release, so that when it is tripped the movement is upwards. When the sapling is released and swings upwards it carries the stone in the pouch, and coming suddenly to the stop the stone is thrown from the forks forward to the path.

Pig Stabber

NOTE.—This is a very dangerous trap to leave set where it might injure anyone walking along the path. Warning notices should be set on

A site is selected where two trees grow close together near the path the animal uses. A very springy sapling is cut, and lashed between the two trees so that when unbent it reaches to the centre of the track. To the end of this sapling a sharp dagger-like knife, or failing that, a pointed spear of hardwood is lashed. If wood is used, make sure that it is straight grained, and harden the end by scorching over fire. Sharpen to a good point.

The sapling is bent back as far as your strength will

permit and note where the bent back of the sapling comes to above the ground. A few feet back from this point set the sticks for the release given in the snare 'Toggle and Bait Stick'. To the bait stick of this release tie the trip cord, and run this along the ground to the position at which the bent sapling came when the head was straight over the path. The trip here should be very light and raised a few inches above the ground. The animal passing along the trap in either direction releases the trip, and the sapling is released with the spear.

Caution. Remember that this is a very dangerous trap and if used, warning notices must be placed either side.

Box Traps to Catch Animals Alive

DOUBLE-ENDED PEN WITH SELF-LOCKING DOORS

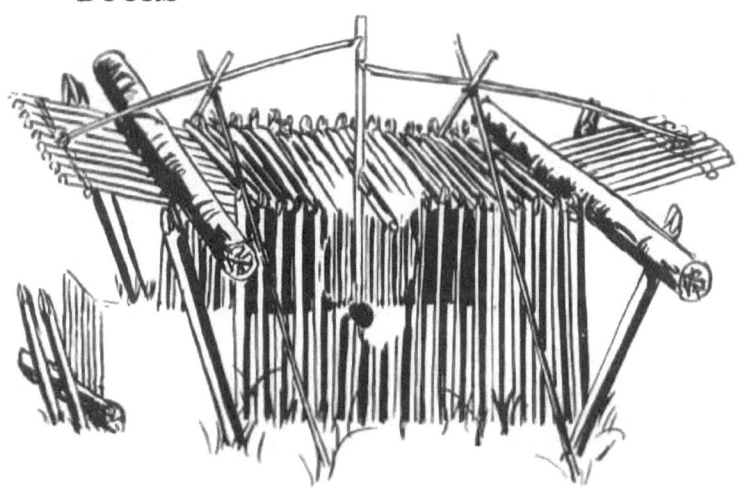

A strong pen of the size required is constructed with both ends left open. The pen is completely roofed over, and in the centre, one of the cross sticks across the roof is squared on one side and on its under surface. The cross pieces at the extreme ends are secured extra strongly to take two drop doors. A couple of inches beyond the line of the side walls, and about three inches from the end uprights very strong stakes are driven into the ground at an angle leaning away from the line of the pen. The two doors are made and hinged with loops of rope or strong vine to the end crossbars, across either end of the pen. On the outside, two support sticks are crossed about seven to ten inches above the roof of the pen. The release sticks are sharpened at one end to a chisel edge, and the bait stick is cut with a squared step about eighteen inches below its top (the square face at the lower end). Ten to twelve inches above this and parallel to the first cut, two square-nicked cuts are made with the squared face on the top side of the cut. The trap is set by putting the bait stick between the crossbars and engaging the squared cut of the bait stick with the squared face of the cross bar. The chisel end of one of the release sticks is placed in one of the top nicks of the bait stick, and the other end between two of the crossbars of the door. The release stick sits on the support sticks as a fulcrum. This is repeated at the other door. Both doors are now raised, and any disturbance of the bait stick will release the support sticks and the doors will drop. The locking device is effected by cutting two heavy poles about eight to ten inches longer than the trap is wide. These are laid across the top end of either door. When the doors start to drop the logs roll down the falling doors, and jam against the outward leaning stakes, thus wedging the doors tight.

Portable Box Traps

EXTERNAL RELEASE

A box is made exactly similar to the box trap on the following page. A hole is bored in the roof 3 inches from the closed-in end. The bait wire is made with an eye at the top, and about four inches below this another eye, and the hooked portion for the bait some eight or ten inches below this lower eye. With this release the cross wire is placed through the lower eye, with the top eye above the roof of the box. The bait is fastened to the hook inside the box, and the release wire secured with its own eye to the top eye, and its farther end lying longways along the roof with the end itself in a small hole through the bottom of the drop door, and in such a position that it holds the door up. When the animal takes the bait, and drags backward with it, the top end of the bait

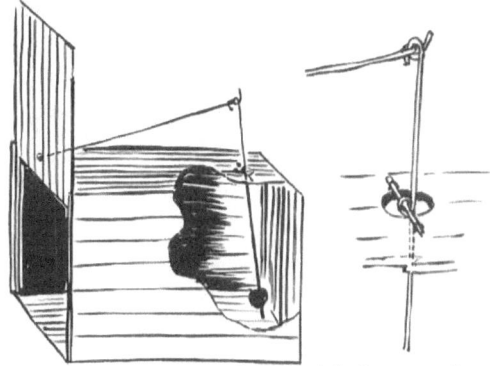

wire is forced to the rear, and so withdraws the wire at the door from the hole and allows the door to stop, imprisoning the animal.

INTERNAL RELEASE

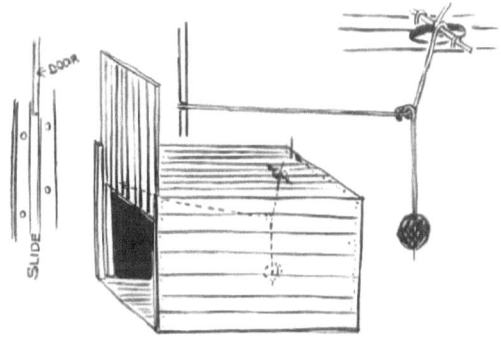

A stout box of a size suitable for the animal to be trapped is made. To one end a sliding door is fitted. This door must slide up and down easily between two grooves. On the inside of the door, and near the lower end a small hole is bored for about a quarter of an inch in depth.

On the roof of the box, about three inches from the closed-in end a hole about one inch diameter is bored right through the wood. The release mechanism is made by taking a piece of stiff wire (8 gauge), bending an eye in it at the head, and another eye about six inches lower down, and immediately below this lower eye bending the wire in a wide hook, and cutting it off at the end of the hook. Through the top eye another short piece of wire is passed (with the eye in the centre of the hole in the roof) and the short piece of wire lying parallel to the end of the box, it is secured in position with a staple at either end. Another piece of wire is fastened to the lower eye, now inside the box. This piece of wire must be just so long that when the hook is slightly forward, the piece of wire will engage in the hole which was bored in a short distance in the foot of the door.

The trap is baited by securing the bait to the U-shaped hook on the lower end of the wire inside the trap. The free end of the inner piece of wire is placed inside the hole at the lower end of the door. When the animal disturbs the bait the wire holding up the door is withdrawn, and the door drops, imprisoning the animal.

INSIDE STICK RELEASE

There are occasions when a piece of wire may be unobtainable, then this internal stick release can be improvised. The box is made as for the preceding portable box traps, complete with sliding door. For the release three forked sticks are used with the bait stick, which should have a fork at one end. The length of the three forked sticks should be such that two of them are equal and about three-quarters the height of the inside of the box, and the third should be about half the height. The fork at the end of the bait stick is so trimmed that one end of the fork is about an inch shorter than the other. Setting is effected by placing the bottom of the door on the longer of the two arms of the fork bait stick with the shorter arm in the inside of the door. The two longer forks are set near the end of the box, their forks holding the far end of the bait stick a few inches from its very end. The shorter forked stick is placed with its fork over the farthest end of the bait stick, and its other end against the roof. The bait is secured to the bait stick near the first pair of forks. When the animal takes the bait, it either disturbs the setting of the forked sticks which hold the slide door up, or it pushes the forked end of the bait stick inwards and allows the door to drop.

LOG ROOFED PEN

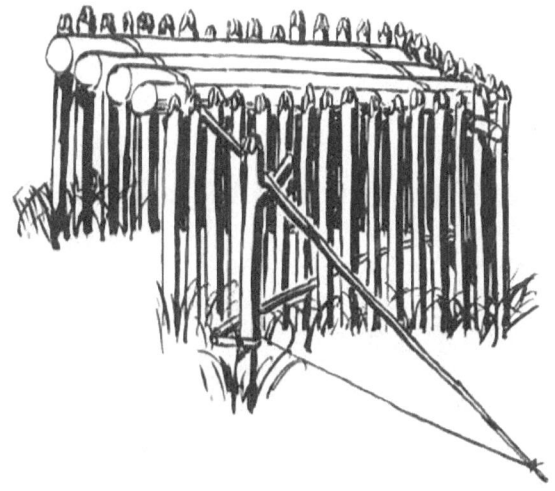

A pen of adequate size for the animal to be trapped is strongly constructed. The pen is built with two sides and one end only. Across the closed end a strong cross bar is secured. Release of the log weighted roof is by means of a toggle and bait stick almost exactly similar to the toggle release of the logfall. A forked stick is stood upright a few-inches from one side of the trap at the open end. Across the fork a supporting stick is placed with the end of the roof logs resting on it. To the far end of this supporting stick a length of cord is fastened, and to the end of this a short toggle stick is tied. The end of the toggle stick is pressed against the bait stick, which in turn is pressed against the stakes opposite and at the far end of the pen. Disturbance of the bait stick releases its engagement with the toggle stick, which in turn releases the support stick and the roof falls heavily, imprisoning the animal in the pen.

FALLING CAGE, FIGURE 4 RELEASE

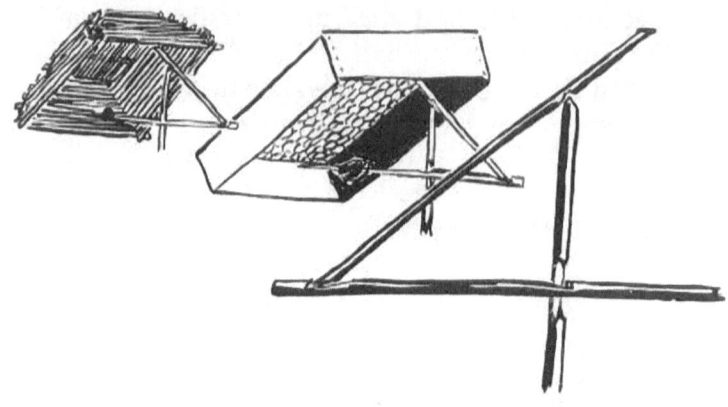

A cage, either of sticks lashed to a pyramidal or other suitable shape, or of boxwood, or netting is made of adequate size. Release is effected by means of the figure 4 release. This is an excellent trap for ground feeding birds, and if the ground is baited with grain, or small fruits it is a certain trap for pigeons. The upright stick is cut with a chisel edge at the top, and a few inches from the bottom end it is squared on all four sides. The support stick is sharpened to a chisel edge at one end, and where it will cross the top of the upright, a nick is cut parallel to the chisel edge. The bait stick has a nick undercut at the thickest end, and at the place where it will cross the upright it has a cut made with a square face at the end of the cut farthest from the undercut nick. Setting is effected by standing the upright in front of the trap, and placing the support stick with its nick on the chisel edge of the upright, and the upper end supporting the raised edge of the box. The chisel end of the support stick is placed in the undercut nick at the end of the bait stick. The squared cut in the bait stick should now engage with a squared face of the support stick, and with the baited end of the stick well under the trap.

Wire Cage Trap for Rabbits

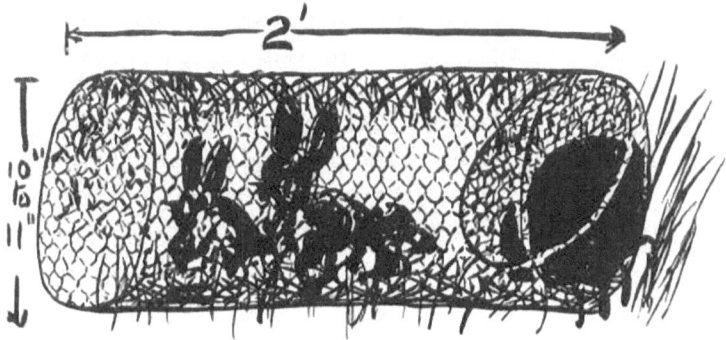

One of the most effective methods of catching rabbits is by means of a wire netting cage trap set at the entrance to one of the burrows of the warren. The warren itself is carefully examined, and a suitable burrow selected for the site of the trap. All the other burrows are covered with a layer of paper stuffed into the hole and packed for a few inches with earth. At the selected burrow the trap, simply made in the form of a long cage of wire netting with one end closed and with the other end as a wire door suspended from the top of the cage and falling so that it can be pushed easily into the trap but when it falls cannot be pushed outwards.

The rabbits in the warren coming to the burrows stuffed with paper are disturbed and suspicious of the rustle of the paper, and come finally to the burrow which has the wire cage in front of it. They push forward into the opening and the door lifting inwards permits them to enter the cage. When they are inside the cage the door drops behind them, and there is no escape back into the safety of the burrow. Ten or twelve rabbits a night can be taken from a warren with this trap, which is far preferable on humanitarian grounds to the steel-jawed commercial trap so commonly used.

Net Trap for Catching Animals Alive

An alternative to the box type traps for catching animals alive and without injury can be devised by using many of the releases shown, in combination with the pull of a springy sapling. For purposes of demonstration in these pages one such arrangement is shown above. The net, of suitable size and strength, is spread on the ground and the centre is baited, as for any of the spring snares. When the release is effected the four corners of the net, being tied to the main rope holding down the sapling, are suddenly pulled upwards, enfolding the captured animal in the net without injuring it in any way. The animal in its struggles gets its legs through the mesh of the net, and so cannot climb out or tear the net to escape. It may chew its way out if the net is left unattended for any length of time.

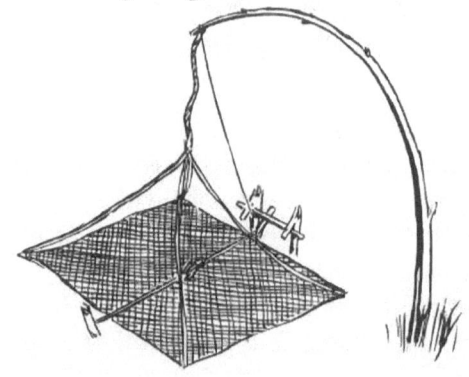

Use of a Rat-Trap or a Fish Hook for Ducks or Geese

Select an area where, by the tracks and droppings, you know wild duck or geese feed. An ordinary rat trap, baited with a frog, and securely tied to a convenient log or stake is set either on a stone, or some place where it will lie flat and secure. The bird, in taking the bait, springs the trap, which cutting into its skull kills instantly. The fish-hook baited with a frog is tied to a stake by a short length of line. When the bird takes the bait it is hooked and held for killing. Alternatively, the cord from the fish-hook can be tied to a heavy stone, which, dislodged when the bird takes the bait, falls into the water and drowns the bird.

These two methods of catching wild birds are illegal in many countries, and are decidedly unsporting. They would be a legitimate method of getting game for food only in emergency. Another method frequently used by poachers for killing pheasants, pigeons and grain-eating birds is to soak split peas and then put thin wire through them, leaving about 1/8-inch of wire projecting from either side of the peas. The bird pick up the peas. The wire pierces their crops and they die quickly. This method is strictly illegal and destructive, and should never be used. You may find such 'doctored' peas or grain in an area and, if so, immediately inform the nearest game warden or ranger. Vandals who destroy bird life by such means as this are severely punished in most civilised countries.

Blind Roller for an Automatic Fisherman

A discarded blind roller is fixed, with its bracket to either a pole or the convenient branch of a tree. The fishing line is secured to the roller, and then, with the roller pawl engaged, the line is pulled so that it touches the water, or until the tension on the line is considered to be adequate. The roller is removed from the brackets and rewound by hand. This will give tension to the line to play the fish. The baited hook is lowered into the water, making sure that the pawls are engaged. When the fish strikes it will disengage the pawls, and the tension of the wound-up roller will play the fish, finally bringing it almost to the surface of the water. The lazy fisherman simply has to unhook his catch, rebait the line and cast in for his second catch.

In general it is better to set the blind roller on to a pole which can be set horizontally above the water, and lashed to a convenient tree or stake, than to set the roller onto a branch. It is easier to remove the catch and reset, and also the pole with the roller blind can be moved to other locations.

Fish Traps

ARROWHEAD TIDAL FISH TRAP SUITABLE FOR AREAS OF FOUR TO SIX FEET TIDES

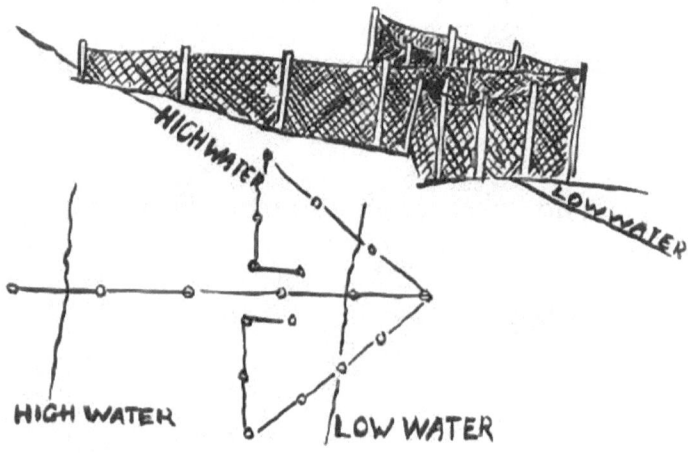

This is a permanent trap and will always ensure a plentiful supply of fish at all seasons. Select a site on an estuary or sheltered cove where the beach slopes fairly evenly. At this site run a fence of wire netting out at low tide so that the top of the fence will be a few inches above high water level, and the lower end will have a foot to eighteen inches of water at low tide. From the low water end of the fence run back two wing fences each at an angle of about forty-five degrees. These two wing fences should come halfway up to the high level water mark, and from the shore end of these two wing fences run two short fences parallel to the beach and stopping with a turnback to the arrowhead about two yards short of the centre fence.

The fish come in to the beach on the rising tide and feed swimming along the beach. They come to the central fence, and turn along it to the deep water, reach the corner at the deep water end and are turned by the wing fence, and again by the fence parallel to the beach. You can clear the trap at low tide, taking from it only those fish which you need. This trap has the advantage of only catching fish of good size, and not killing anything which may not be required for food. There will always be fish left in the pool at low water, and some of these are bound to find their way out to deep water at the next rise of the tide.

TIDAL ROCK POOL TRAP

A site is selected where there are a number of rock pools well covered at high tide, and barely dry at low tide. One such rock pool is selected, and heavily baited with such food as crushed up shell fish, small portions of freshly killed fish, crushed up rock crabs and the like. Across the normal opening of the rock pool a wall of rocks is built so that the top of the wall will be a few inches below the water at high tide.

This should be done at a time when there is a low tide at dusk and dawn.

The fish, feeding at night on the rising tide, come to the rock pool, drawn there by the lures and baits lying on the bottom. With the fall of the tide they are trapped until the next full tide and if the rock pool you have selected is not too large at low tide you can easily collect your catch with a scoop net.

CRAB OR LOBSTER NET

Make a circular wire hoop, three or four feet in diameter, and sew a piece of net or thin bagging around the edges so that there is a foot or so sag. To the wire hoop, tie three or four short lengths of rope, and join these together about three feet above the hoop. These cords from the hoop are tied to the hoisting rope, which can either be buoyed or tied to a convenient post or piece of rock, depending upon the location where the trap is being used. The bottom of the net is weighted with a piece of rock, and baited with a few fish-heads or portions of small fish. These must be securely tied to the bottom of the net.

The net is lowered into the sea, and left for about two hours. Pull it up swiftly, and any crabs or lobsters which have been feeding on the bait will be caught in the sag.

For lobsters, set the net on a rocky weedy bottom, or for crabs, on a sandy bottom, preferably not far from an underwater reef.

DRUM NET

A drum net is simply a wire cage with inverted cone shaped entrance at either end. These doors lead inwards and the fish swimming in through the cones are held securely inside the trap. A drummet can either be set in mid-stream, or dropped down into a deep pool of a nearby river, or set off a rocky ledge at the seaside.

A drum net must be baited to be effective, and almost any old bait will do, fish-heads, inedible varieties of fish, large shellfish or other bait will all attract fish to the feast.

Make your drum net large and weight the bottom with a couple of heavy stones, also use a large-size mesh so that small fish can swim out freely. A drum net is an ideal way to ensure a regular supply of fresh fish.

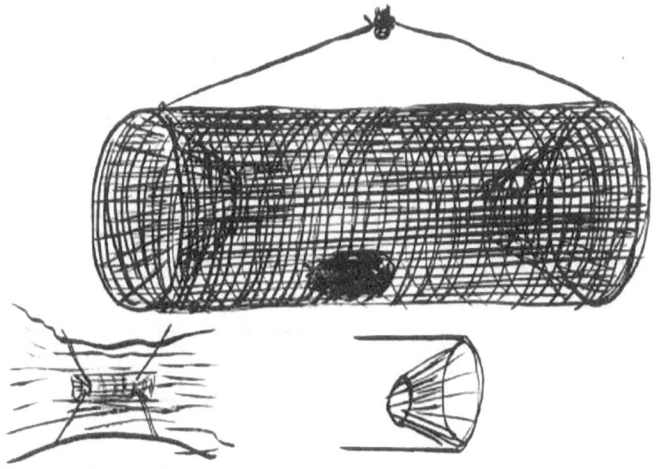

SNARE FOR LOBSTERS OR YABBIES

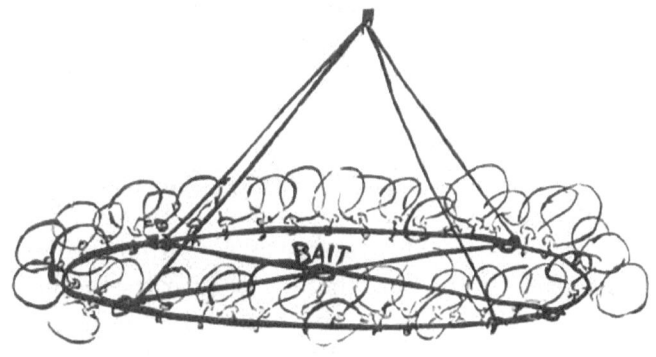

A circle of heavy gauge wire (8 gauge) is made. The circle should be from 12" to 15" across. To support its shape two cross wires are secured.

Around the circle of wire a series of running nooses are tied. The noose need be no more than 2 inches across. Heavy nylon fishing line is excellent for this. These nooses should be about 1" to 1½" apart around the circle.

The bait is tied in the centre where the supporting cross wires pass each other.

Three or four cords tied to the circle are joined to a central rope which is buoyed to mark its position.

This is an excellent lobster snare.

HOLLOW LOG TRAP FOR FRESH WATER FISH

The fact that fish cannot swim backwards is made use of in this hollow log trap. A hollow log, not too large in diameter is covered at one end with a piece of wire netting or other material which will allow a free flow of water. A sling is made in such a manner that when the rope is pulled to lift the trap to the surface it will tilt the hollow log so that the wired-in end is lowest. The bait is put in a few inches from this closed end and the trap lowered into a convenient pool or off a rock ledge.

The fish swimming about in the stream will scent the bait, and eventually find their way into the hollow log by means of the open end. If the hollow in the log is not too large the fish will be unable to turn around to swim out, and as a result will be trapped in the hollow. The open end of the hollow log should always be upstream, otherwise the current may wash the fish free.

A similar method of catching smaller fish is possible with an open-necked pickle bottle. The bait, such as a piece of dough, or other food, is stuck at the lower end of the bottle. The bottle is placed in shallow water, taking care to see that all air is first removed before setting the bottle in position. Small fish such as sand mullet, whiting, etc., will swim into the bottle, and cannot return. This is a good way to catch small fish for bait.

STICK SNARE FOR SURFACE FEEDING FISH

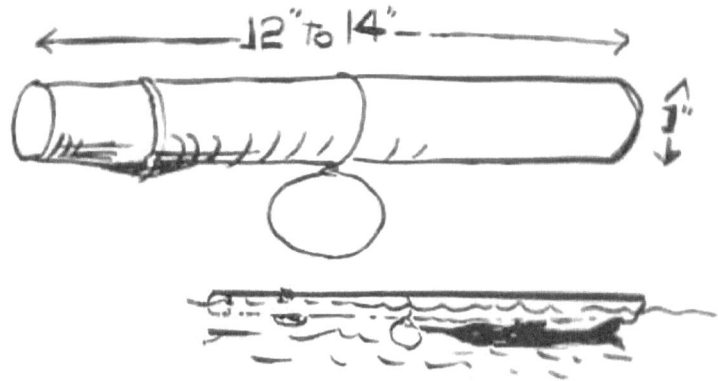

Surface feeding fish may be snared by means of a noose set on the underside of a weighted stick. The stick should be ten to twelve inches long, and on one side a small chip of stone is secured, either by tying or by slightly splitting the stick and driving the chip of stone into the split. A noose of gut, horsehair, or other thin material is tied so that the noose is on the same side as the stone chip. A number of these noose sticks are made and thrown into the sea from a rocky promontory. Surface feeding fish such as Long Toms and Garfish take cover beneath any debris floating on the surface of the sea. This is their protection against sea birds from above, and other bigger fish from deeper water. They will hide under the noose sticks, and in time either their bills or tails will become caught in the noose. Their struggles against the noose tire them out, and the wash of the surf takes them in to the beach. A couple of hours after you have thrown the noose sticks into the sea they will have drifted in to the wash at the beach and you can recover the sticks and any fish which have become snared in the nooses.

LOBSTER OR CRAYFISH POT

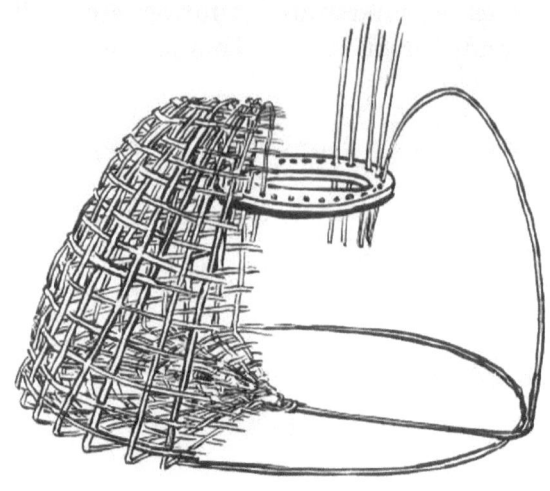

A board about one foot square, by one inch thick, has a circle drawn on one side. The diameter of the circle is about eight inches. Quarter-inch holes are bored around the circle. These holes are about an inch apart. Five-foot lengths of cane are put into each of these holes, and about three or four inches above the board start weaving split cane, so that the shape is like a wide funnel. The upright canes are gradually bent further and further with this weaving till they come right over and down, when the whole working is turned upside down for greater convenience. At the base, which should be about two feet from the top and about three feet across the circle, turn the canes sharply in to the centre of the circle. This, when the lobster pot is turned right way up in the water, is the bottom of the trap.

Weight the bottom with a heavy stone, and bait with old fish heads or other fish bait, and lower the lobster pot into a rocky weedy position. Lobsters live in caves in the rocks, and generally in colonies. The hoisting rope for the pot must be buoyed with a marker so that you can find it again. The pot may take a few days to 'weather' after you have first made it. Several such pots will secure you a fair supply of lobsters or crayfish.

Improvised Fish-Hook Made From Thorns

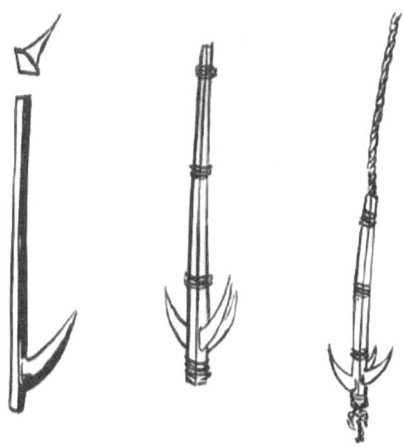

Three long and strong thorns are cut with about two inches of wood left above the upward curve of the thorn, and about a quarter inch below the end of the wood of the thorn. Make sure the thorns are long, hard and sharp. The wood section is pared down with a sharp knife so that the angle is about 120 degrees. If this is done correctly the three pieces of wood with the thorns can be fitted together to make a three-pronged hook. The wood is strongly bound with tough fibre thread at least twice on the shank, and once below. If possible it is advisable to bring the line, or at least a short length (for a cast) down the centre where the three pieces of wood join. This cast should be finished off with a thumb knot at the butt of the hook so that it cannot be pulled through.

Such hooks as this are quite as efficient as the steel hook, and can be easily made by anyone with careful fingers.

Fishing Spears

The best spearing is over shallow sandy shallows at night with an acetylene torch or very powerful five or six cell electric torch. With fish spearing the aim is to pin the fish down with the spear rather than thrust at the fish. Move the spear slowly till it is over the fish and then jab suddenly in the strike. Fish spearing by day can be either done from a boat or raft or coracle, or from a rocky ledge. In any case you will need a sea glass or underwater goggles so that you can see clearly without any interruption by surface ripple. A sea glass can be made by cutting the bottom out of a tin and simply looking through the hole the tin provides. This will protect the water within the tin from surface ripple. Or, better still, you can put a glass bottom to the tin and secure it with sticking plaster or scotch tape. When fishing from a boat, spear as nearly vertical as possible. In spearing for fish move slowly and quietly, and allow for the angle of distortion of the water. Remember that fish have a natural protective colouring and at first they will be difficult to see. They are easiest to detect when they move, or by their shadow against the sea bottom. Fish spears should be multi-pronged for greater efficiency, and, if made of wire are more certain if barbed.

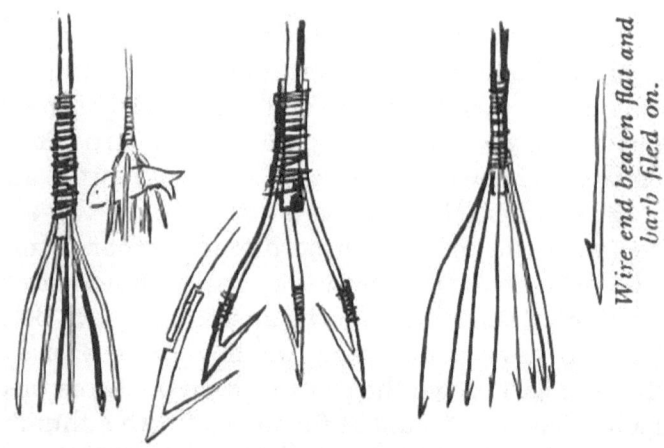

Fire-hardened sticks.   *Barbed trident.*   *Barbed heavy wire.*

Wire end beaten flat and barb filed on.

Baited Float Stick

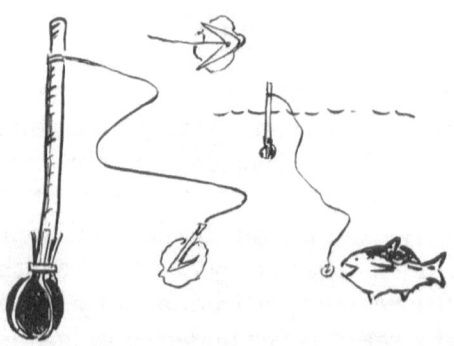

An effective method of fishing with float sticks in fairly calm water or off beaches where there is a set inshore to the beach is possible by constructing a number of 'float sticks' to which a stout short length of fishing line is attached, with either a baited hook or a boomerang-shaped piece of bone or shell baited as for a hook. These float sticks are made about two feet long, and on one end a fairly heavy stone is attached by means of a couple of straps of bark strips of cane enclosing the stone, and bound to the stick. This weight will make the stick stand upright in the water. To the top end of the stick the line is attached, and this should be about two to three yards in length. The farthest end of the cord carries the baited hook or piece of bone. These sticks are thrown into the water and allowed to drift. The fish taking the bait is hooked either by the hook or by the boomerang, and struggling against the drag of the bait stick, exhausts itself so that the drift or current takes it in its course. It is necessary if you are using this method of fishing to watch the direction of drift or current and know whereabouts to look for the sticks some hours after you have cast them into the water.

Tracks, Baits and Lures

Trapping calls not only for a knowledge of the mechanics and construction of a particular trap or snare, but also for an intelligent knowledge of the habits of the animal to be captured.

This knowledge can be gained by observation of its movements and its feeding habits, and of course by its tracks. For example, you know that all animals with cloven hooves are grazing (ground feeding) animals, but did you realise that all animals which leave the track of a thumb, or even two thumbs, are all tree-climbing animals, or that all animals which burrow show the track of their digging claws quite clearly? Similarly all animals which leave pad-like tracks are carnivorous, that is, flesh eaters.

The same principle can be read into birds' tracks. Hopping birds are generally insect eaters, tracks of walking birds show they may be grain, insect or flesh eaters, and when you learn to recognise the talons of the tracks of a hawk or crow from the insect-digging toe of a lyre bird or an ibis you are well on the way to being able to' read correctly the story book of tracks and trails. All the traps given in this book are ineffective unless they are sited correctly and baited properly.

As a human being you regard siting as a matter only for your eyes. You SEE things. You must remember when trapping that wild animals rely much more upon their sense of scent than upon their sense of sight. They 'see' things with their noses, not with their eyes. Your scent if left on a trap will warn an animal of danger. You can destroy this scent by either drowning it, or by scorching the trap to burn it clean, or by allowing it to stand for a long time to 'weather' and so lose the human scent.

Human scent on a trap or snare can be drowned by the use of a stronger scent which is also a 'lure.' A lure is a smell which will attract an animal. Two excellent lures are oil of aniseed and oil of rhodium. Both will attract most bush animals.

Before setting up any trap you would be wise to test bait the locality to find out which baits will attract the animals, and also to find out what creatures are in the locality. To test bait, select your site on a piece of clean dusty ground. Drive fifteen to twenty small stakes into the ground, and attach to each a different bait, some with lures, and some without. Mark each peg with a number, and make a note of the number and the bait which each carried. This work should be done in the afternoon. When you have all the baits fastened to the pegs, brush the ground clean. When you visit the test baited area next morning you will see the tracks of all the creatures that came to it in the evening, during the night and in the early morning. These are the times when all wild animals feed.

The tracks will tell you which animals took the baits, and also what baits were taken, and then, if you make your traps and bait them with the correct baits, they will be effective for you. In general, tree climbing animals will take fruits as a bait, digging animals will take sweet potato or carrot or anv of our edible roots, while flesh eating animals of course will only take flesh. Herbage eaters will often take a cabbage or lettuce leaf as a delicacy and, in many civilised areas, bread will be an effective bait.